A Teacher's Tools

Dava Pressberg

PowerKiDS
press.

New York

Published in 2016 by The Rosen Publishing Group, Inc.
29 East 21st Street, New York, NY 10010

First Edition

Editor: Caitie McAneney
Book Design: Reann Nye

Photo Credits: Cover (woman) wavebreakmedia/Shutterstock.com; cover (background) luminaimages/Shutterstock.com; pp. 5, 9, 20 Monkey Business Images/Shutterstockcom; pp. 6, 21 (planner) MikhailSh/Shutterstock.com; p. 7 racorn/ Shutterstock.com; pp. 8, 21 (pen) leedsn/Shutterstock.com; pp. 10, 21 (highlighter) Evgeny Karandaev/Shutterstock.com; pp. 10, 21 (flags) jesadaphorn/Shutterstock.com; pp. 10, 21 (sticky note) ImagePost/Shutterstock.com; p. 11 Ortis/ Shutterstock.com; pp. 12, 21 (folder) Carolyn Franks/Shutterstock.com; p. 12 (organizational shelf) DenisNata/Shutterstock.com; pp. 13, 19 Tyler Olson/Shutterstock.com; p. 15 Yellow Dog Productions/Digital Vision/Getty Images; pp. 16, 21 (whiteboard) piotr_pabijan/Shutterstock.com; p. 17 © iStockphoto.com/4x6; pp. 18, 21 (laptop) Igor Lateci/Shutterstock.com; pp. 18, 21 (desktop computer) Denis Rozhnovsky/Shutterstock.com; p. 21 (gradebook) © iStockphoto.com/Korovin; p. 21 (magnet) sil63/ Shutterstock.com; p. 21 (loose-leaf paper) Paul Vasarhelyi/Shutterstock.com; p. 21 (binder) nito/Shutterstock.com; p. 21 (notebook) valzan/Shutterstock.com; p. 21 (bulletin board) Texturis/Shutterstock.com; p. 21 (blackboard) mexrix/Shutterstock.com; p. 21 (textbook) Seregam/Shutterstock.com; p. 21 (workbook) Jiri Hera/Shutterstock.com; p. 21 (copier) Vereshchagin Dmitry/ Shutterstock.com; p. 21 (tablet) cretolamna/shutterstock.com; p. 21 (pencil) Hayati Kayhan/Shutterstock.com; p. 21 (interactive whiteboard) RTimages/Shutterstock.com; p. 22 Chris Howey/Shutterstock.com.

Cataloging-in-Publication Data

Pressberg, Dava.
A teacher's tools / by Dava Pressberg.
p. cm. — (Community helpers and their tools)
Includes index.
ISBN 978-1-4994-0855-3 (pbk.)
ISBN 978-1-4994-0859-1 (6 pack)
ISBN 978-1-4994-0904-8 (library binding)
1. Teachers — Juvenile literature. I. Pressberg, Dava. II. Title.
LB1775.2 P744 2016
371.1'00973—d23

Manufactured in the United States of America

CPSIA Compliance Information: Batch #WS15PK: For Further Information contact Rosen Publishing, New York, New York at 1-800-237-9932

Contents

Teaching Tools

Teachers give students the tools they need to learn about important subjects, such as reading, math, and science. That makes them important community helpers! However, their job is far from easy. Teachers also need tools to teach students important skills that will help them be successful.

How do teachers do their jobs? Teachers go to school for a long time to learn how to teach others. They read about subjects to become **experts** on them.

TOOL TIME!

Some teachers use textbooks to teach their students. Textbooks are full of facts about a certain subject. They make teaching and learning a subject as easy as possible.

Books are some of the greatest tools teachers have.

Books and More Books!

Textbooks aren't the only kinds of books teachers use. In some subjects, such as math and English, teachers might give their students workbooks. Workbooks are books students can write in. This is helpful for math because it lets students work out their math problems on paper.

Teachers also use notebooks. They might have a notebook where they write notes about lessons or grades. They might also give out notebooks so students can write in them.

TOOL TIME!

A planner is a kind of notebook that has a space for each day. Planners help teachers keep track of their lessons throughout the week.

planner

Some teachers use gradebooks to keep track of their students' scores. Today, most teachers keep their students' scores saved in a special program on their computer.

Writing Tools

Notebooks and loose-leaf paper, or individual lined pages, are great for note taking. Teachers and students also need writing tools to do that. Teachers and students often use pencils to write notes and work out math problems. Pencils often have erasers on them, so it's okay to make mistakes when writing.

Teachers also use pens for writing. They might give their students pens when they're **confident** there will be few mistakes in their writing.

TOOL TIME!

Some teachers like to use pens with special ink that can be erased.

pens

Some pencils have to be sharpened, so teachers will need a pencil sharpener. Electric pencil sharpeners use a spinning blade to sharpen the pencil. Some pencil sharpeners need to be turned by hand.

Staying Organized

Teachers have many things to keep track of! They need to keep track of their students' homework, tests, grades, and the lesson plans that help them teach their subject. There are many tools teachers can use to help **organize** their papers.

Sometimes teachers need to organize **information** in a book or in papers. They can use highlighters to mark important pieces of information. Highlighters are markers with bright, light colors. To keep track of test scores, a teacher might highlight just the test scores in their gradebook.

flags   sticky note   highlighter

TOOL TIME!

Sticky notes sometimes come in the form of tiny flags. These colorful flags help teachers mark an important page in a group of papers.

Teachers can also use sticky notes to mark important pages or write notes. Sticky notes are small pieces of paper with a strip of glue on the back.

With so many papers, it's easy to misplace or lose important ones. It's important that teachers file their papers in special places to set them apart from one another. This calls for more tools!

Teachers might use folders to keep papers of the same subject together. For example, a teacher could have one folder for homework pages, one folder for quizzes, and one folder for tests. Teachers can choose certain colors as a code to remember which folder holds which papers.

folders

organizational shelf

TOOL TIME!

Teachers can use special shelves and closets to set their papers and books apart from each other.

Teachers can also put papers in binders. Binders have rings that keep pages in place. Teachers can use paper tools called binder dividers to create sections within the binder.

Post It!

Sometimes teachers have important news or papers they'd like to share with the class. Teachers can use bulletin boards to post paper items, such as **inspirational** sayings, field-trip announcements, or the lunch menu.

Some bulletin boards are made of corkboard, which is a soft, woody matter. Teachers can easily stick pins into corkboard to hang pieces of paper. Bulletin boards help teachers keep students notified, but can also be fun. Teachers sometimes use them to post about someone's birthday or holidays.

TOOL TIME!

Some teachers post notices and other papers on metal surfaces using magnets. Others post important information on a website or send it in an email.

Teachers can use bulletin boards to post pictures and facts that have to do with lessons. This teacher has maps and pictures on her bulletin board.

Sharing and Illustrating

When a teacher teaches a lesson, they often need a surface to share information and **illustrate** their point. Many classrooms have blackboards, also called chalkboards. Blackboards are a dark color, such as black or green, and teachers can draw on them with white or colored chalk. This helps teachers illustrate math problems or write important science facts.

Some classrooms have whiteboards. These are white surfaces that teachers can draw on with erasable markers. Whiteboards help show information like blackboards.

whiteboard

TOOL TIME!

Teachers can use copy machines and scanners to make many copies of one handout.

Teachers can also share information with students by making printed papers to hand out. They can print these using a printer.

17

New Teaching Technology

There are more tools for teachers today than ever before. Perhaps the most important tool is a computer. Teachers use computers to type up their lesson plans and keep track of grades and assignments. They can also use computers to **research** ideas for lessons. They can post grades online and email parents about how their children are doing in class.

Some teachers use special **software** on their computers. Some software helps make vocabulary worksheets, while other software has educational games.

TOOL TIME!

Laptops are computers that open and close like a notebook. They're easy to carry from place to place. Desktop computers are usually bigger and stay in one place.

laptop

desktop computer

Some teachers have tablets to help their students learn. Tablets are small, touchscreen computers. They can hold games, quizzes, and other learning tools.

Blackboards and whiteboards are great tools for sharing information, but they're quickly becoming a thing of the past. Many teachers now have **interactive** whiteboards in their classrooms.

Interactive whiteboards are large screens that connect to a computer. Students and teachers can touch the screen to work on problems, switch to a new image, or illustrate their thoughts. Some teachers have a special tablet that connects to the whiteboard. Students can write or draw on the tablet and the image appears on the whiteboard.

A Teacher's Tools

books

textbooks

workbook

gradebook

notebooks

planner

loose-leaf paper

new technology

laptop

desktop computer

tablet

interactive whiteboard

organizing

highlighter

sticky note

flags

binder

folders

sharing information

magnets

whiteboard

blackboard

copy machine

bulletin board

writing

pencil

pens

21

Around the Classroom

Different teachers use different kids of tools. Art teachers use paint and clay to make art **projects**. Technology teachers use hammers and screwdrivers to teach students how to build. Music teachers use drums and guitars to teach students music. Gym teachers use basketballs and soccer balls.

Teachers' tools help teachers make learning fun. Some tools help teachers stay organized, while others help them share information with their classes. Next time you're in class, look around your classroom. What important teacher tools do you see?

Glossary

confident: Believing one can succeed.

expert: Someone who has a special skill or knowledge.

illustrate: To create pictures that help explain something.

information: Knowledge gained from study or observation.

inspirational: Having features or properties that make someone want to do or create something.

interactive: Having to do with a two-way system of actions between a computer and a user.

organize: To put together in an orderly way.

project: A task.

research: Studying to find something new.

software: A program that runs on a computer and does certain tasks.

Index

Websites

Due to the changing nature of Internet links, PowerKids Press has developed an online list of websites related to the subject of this book. This site is updated regularly. Please use this link to access the list: www.powerkidslinks.com/cht/tea